SHADES

Also by Heather McHugh

Dangers
A World of Difference
To the Quick
D'Après Tout: Poems by Jean Follain (a translation)

WESLEYAN POETRY

SHADES

Heather McHugh

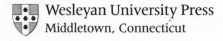
Wesleyan University Press
Middletown, Connecticut

Poems in this book originally appeared in these magazines and
anthologies: *Boston Review, Exquisite Corpse, Harvard Magazine,
Michigan Quarterly Review, New American Poets of the 80's, Painted
Bride Quarterly, Sonora Review, Threepenny Review*. "From 20,000
Feet" was reprinted as a broadside by Northouse & Northouse.

All inquiries and permissions requests should be addressed to the
Publisher, Wesleyan University Press, 110 Mt. Vernon Street,
Middletown, Connecticut 06457

Distributed by Harper & Row Publishers, Keystone Industrial Park,
Scranton, Pennsylvania 18512

LIBRARY OF CONGRESS CATALOGING-IN-PUBLICATION DATA

McHugh, Heather, 1948–
  Shades / Heather McHugh.—1st ed.
    p.   cm.
  ISBN 0-8195-2142-6 ISBN 0-8195-1137-4 (pbk.)
  I. Title.
PS3563.A311614S5   1988   87-21179
811'.54—dc19   CIP

Manufactured in the United States of America

FIRST EDITION

WESLEYAN POETRY

*For Raya Garbousova Biss
who taught me
life is too short to be small*

Contents

Mox Nox   ix

I
20-200 on 747   3

II
What Hell Is   7
Third Person Neuter   9
By Faith Not Sight   10
Unspeakable   12
This   14
Round Time   15
Point of Needle   17

III
Place Where Things Got   21
One Moon in Binoculars   23
Primate Song   24
Inflation   25
To Have To   26
At Sprecht Academy   27
Autobiography with Suspended Period   28
No Place   30
The Lyricist's Lament   31
The Oven Loves the TV Set   32
Unfamiliar   34
Artifactual   35
We Had Words   37
Who Made Her   38
Earthmoving Malediction   40
It Is Unhealthy Not to Die   41
Where   42
ID   43

Gospel According to Virginia   44

Hole Filler   45

Earmarks   46

Our Element   47

Forecast   49

IV

Shades   53

Spilled   54

A Mother   56

Not a Sin   57

In Primary Colors   58

The Typewriter's the Kind   59

Hard   60

Melted Money   61

Labor   62

Stairwell   63

Two Humans Being   64

With You Gone   66

As It Was in the Beginning   67

Thought of Night   69

How Come: A Book of Numbers   70

From 20,000 Feet   71

Mox Nox

"Ultima Multis" (The last, for many)
Inscription on a sundial in the Hautes-Pyrénées

Hasten slowly, the sundial said.
Day and die are cast together.

Covering, I discover
said the dial. All things are dream.

They fly as you stand still.
You may know hours

but you do not know your hour:
light is shed

but the last
is hidden.

Shade warns shade
the sundial said.

20-200 on 747

There is rain on the glass but it all disappears
when I look toward the curve on the world.
(The here and now is clear, I mean, so we
can't see it.) In an airplane, chance

encounters always ask, So what
are your poems about? They're about
their business, and their father's business and their
monkey's uncle, they're about

how nothing is about, they're not
about about. This answer drives them
back to the snack tray every time.
Phil Fenstermacher, for example, turns up

perfectly clear in my memory, perfectly attentive to
his Vache Qui Rit, that saddest cheese. And now an interlude
    while we
commiserate: it takes what might
be years to open life's array

of incidental parcels—mysteries
of red strips, tips, and strings, the tricks
of tampons, lips of band-aids, perforated notches on
detergent boxes, spatial reasoning milk-carton quiz and subtle

teleologies of toilet paper.
Mister Fenstermacher is relieved
to fill his mind with the immediate
and masterable challenge of the cheese

after his brief and chastening foray
into the social arts. We part
before we part; indeed
we part before we meet. I sense

the French philosophers nearby,
I hope not in the cockpit (undermining
meaning, as they do, or testing aerial translation's
three degrees). They think

we're sunk, we're sunk, in our little
container, our story
of starting and stopping. Just
whose story is this anyway? Out of my mind

whose words emerge? Is there a self the self
surpasses? (Look at your glasses, someone
whispers. Maybe the world
is speckled by

your carelessness and not its nature.
Look at your glasses, if you want
to see.) Who says? We're not
alone, the town down there

grows huge, one tiny runway will
engulf us. Is the whisperer
Phil Fenstermacher, getting a last word in
before the craft alights? I look

at my glasses. I see
what he means. They're a sight.

What Hell Is

March, 1985

Your father sits inside
his spacious kitchen, corpulent
and powerless. Nobody knows
how your disease is spread; it came
from love, or some
such place. Your father's bought
with forty years of fast talk, door-to-door,
this fancy house you've come home now to die in.
Let me tell you what
hell is, he says: I got this
double fridge all full of food
and I can't let my son go in.

*

Your parents' friends
stop visiting. You are a damper on
their spirits. Every day you feel
more cold (no human being
here can bear
the thought—it's growing
huge, as you grow thin).
Ain't it a bitch, you say, this
getting old? (I'm not sure
I should laugh. No human being
helps, except
suddenly, simply
Jesus: him you hold.)

*

We're not allowed
to touch you if you weep or bleed.
Applying salve to sores that cannot heal
your brother wears a rubber glove.
With equal meaning, cold or kiss
could kill you. Now what do I mean
by love?

*

7

The man who used
to love his looks
is sunk in bone
and looking out.

Framed by immunities
of telephone and lamp
his mouth is shut,
his eyes are dark.

While we discuss despair
he is it, somewhere
in the house. Increasingly
he's spoken of

not with. In kitchen
conferences we come
to terms that we
can bear. But where is he?

In hell, which is
the living room.
In hell, which has
an easy chair.

Third Person Neuter

Is God mad? Was Christ
crazy? Is the truth
the legal truth? (Three PhD's who swear

the human being who believes
a human being God
is what, in fairness, speaking

clinically, we call
a nut.) No jury,
given sacred laws

of science and democracy, would now
forgive so big a claim as Christ's—a claim
for good. (The wounded get

their settlements in millions, not
worlds-without-end.) We think of bliss
as ignorance, and heaven as naïveté: the doctor's

a philosopher, the priest a practicing
apologist. Not one of them
will let me see

with my own eyes my friend again.
When experts gave him time, it made
his luck and language die. What good

was love? It was the ultimate
authority to quit.
He had no use

for flesh at last
and, Christ,
I'm made of it.

By Faith Not Sight

We cannot get
out of ourselves
to be sure
no atom feels, no

heaven comprehends and so
we simply hope.
Our senses (five
or six) describe

ourselves. (Could being be
so numbered?) All the little
strata of the world—the
audible and visible

of frequencies, the
findable and thinkable
of facts—could they
be fashioned

by and for
our expert self-
importances? Somebody
I adored has died

into unbearability.
But where is that?
Is where a narrow
inquiry? We aren't

our lives, or anything we made
in man or camera's image—where
is where itself? Who's
who? The issue's not

rhetorical: exactly what
we most require
we're most required
to give. And even love

(especially love)
became a homelessness.
Now that he's dead
where can I live?

Unspeakable

While he was dying of
everything, inside and out, I caught
in dreams at night some kind of
scale or bark that spread across
my face and arms until
I looked diseased, and knew myself
at last and found
no peace in knowledge, after all.

My friend by contrast I presumed to love
beyond the physical (beyond the dream)
and as he got cadaverous and sore
it made me more devoted than I ever was
in all the days of his untrammelled
vanity. Easy for me
to love while he lost hope,
to dream while he lost face,
and had to undergo again
that painfully unfinished state
a child is made to suffer,
body that won't stay
put or known, its visage
ranging and de-ranging and its self,
at best, at twelve,
tufted with fresh
atrocities of hair. Adults

forget, but not for good.
My friend stopped talking, wrote
a final poem, having shit for subject
and last word. His sister said
his lips turned inside out. The heart keeps
drumming it, and still
I do not understand. What's
dead? what's dead?

*

With eyes in our heads, we are not made
to see ourselves. Instead the hundred people
packed into this flimsy tent
thrill to organs and banners and candies,
agog for antics in a circus animal. The town
is small, the winter long; we crave
exotic incarnation, trains to swing or sway us,
fancy women, or a man miraculous. Instead we get

this painful elephant, put through his paces
on a red footstool, playing the fumbling footman or
terrible tuba, playing the fool; and all around him
hoots and titters start to swell toward derision
and I'll tell you why: thanks
to a bad road diet, and confinement,
and his shitty life, the elephant is defecating now
voluminously out his nether end (how *could* he, everybody gasps)
and all the while waves daintily in front
the scarf, coquettish, meant to make him cute.
He lumbers and revolves, saluting everyone this way
and that; what he can't see
is half the show; and half the audience,
by turns, is treated to the sight
of how the stuff emerges, where it lands.
The snickers are the language of
the animal the animal offends, the one that thinks
it's different. We can't contain ourselves;
the laughs burst out
in spatters from the stands . . .

This

rigid, brown, stick's time
is a long time, by some standards, time
of years, against whose frame, in spring,
obliterating it, bursts forth the vivid
flowering (tissue of verb, most vulnerable,
fastest killed, inside a week) and then

the leaf's somewhat extended
tenderness, its life of months. And underground
the minerals whose lifetimes are
entangled in successive generations of
the hair of roots—the minerals
are moving too, though we

do not believe it (we are so bound up
in chauvinisms of our own
lifetime and flourishing). I try to train
attention past the past or else
ahead of the ahead, till when
is not a question. Qualities

are relative. Some
quicknesses will be unwise, some
mountains flat. It's not
when, what or how we are
that makes one wonder
without end. It's *that*.

Round Time

Looking back, I look
too straight: I can't locate
my old self, young self, you know who—

my one-and-only, be-all-end-all,
my intended and my ex, the one I was
most smitten with. No matter in how many

shots and tones and letters she
was caught, recorded, dated,
lovingly held still or held

important, now
behind the frozen frame she stays
essentially unrememberable—not to be

surrounded, comprehended—even in time
(especially in time).
And if I try to ride the wave without

desire for destination, just
remembering remembering's
design—the feedback slaps me silly, still,

with multiples of ism, replicas of ness—
a busy copy center, Lake Success,
with mirrors posed for turns, returns, diminishing . . .

We are what we are looking for, a sign.

*

My fingers cannot tell themselves
from the electric typewriter. The room will
rise and fall in mind, the bay beyond the window

have its day, whose islands are the islands of
attention—what exists
is mostly lost on us, and this

despite our best
intentions, fastest
memories. As quickly as

this cat leaps up upon the desk
and settles on the
manuscript—

a curve will overcome the line.

Point of Needle

Stitches in hand and birds in time,
the sweet incisions in the wall
above the oven, turkey
laced up homely
like a boot.
Perhaps we're just

too comfortable.
Our prejudice is woven
into common sense and now
cannot tell home from homily,
the future from a fine
domestication (pretty

pillows in the forecast,
silver lining, heaven billed
as easy street). As good
is busy, we keep sewing
angels into orders,
children into little suits

where suitability
holds sway. We measure how they grow
against a wall. But time and size
are our mistakes. Let one child die
before his mother does

and every age of rulers falls away.

Place Where Things Got

I always thought if I could just
remember where I started I
could understand the end. The cat upon my lap
infolds itself, intends itself;
it makes itself a compact package, perfectly adapted to
the transient circumstance of my repose,
and chooses out of live adjacency
best balance, fewest gestures,
all intelligence, no thought.
It wraps the rest around itself and settles.

For a time its engine runs
continuous, it bumbles and it hums and drones
and then slows down, so little
interludes of stiller stuff occur, some
quietude in patches, here and there, and then
another strength of hum crops up to just
drop off, drop deep and deeper in
to dream, to stir,
to dream, till only
little nubs of noise arise, the
intermittent particles of purr . . .

*

When moments hadn't melted
into ages yet, my sister Jan and I
would grind the sounds of sentences
down past the word to syllables,
the syllables to letters and
the letters into even less:
the grindstone was the voice's slow control;
you spoke so gradually symbol turned
to substance, curve to its
constituents; you shifted rpm until
the voice was gravel and the gravel grain and then
the particles themselves became distinct. If you
could utter utterances slow enough you found
the sand inside a saying, molecules like those

Superman is made of, held up close (as duplicated
supermen will be, by little people).
Grown-ups wouldn't tell us
what is IN a loaf of time or life of story, what's inside
a voice, in other words—away from what
the English teachers wanted and away
from what the elders took for granted,
what's *in* there, aside
from coins of meaning? That is why

we took the trail of crumbs, broke breadstuff down,
backtracked from mines of money toward the mill
where dough turned into grain and grain
to seed and seed to cell and there
beyond iotas of the minuscule we found
a place where things got huge again.

One Moon in Binoculars

How could this homely instrument
have power to pull
the whole moon closer,
hold ten textures in
the intimacy of a glance?
The silvers tremble severally
splashed and sanded,
spine-wise, spidery,
in sharp and shadowed
pocks upon the plain. The view

is black and white, but brighter than TV,
clearer than sand in a glass of vodka,
shivering, with each
detail distilled
down to the pebbles
of ocular grain. To cast an eye
across its wild serenities
is to be glad

you cannot see that otherworldly flag
(our worldly flag, that is). They stuck it
flat and stiff up there, because
there is no wind. They made
an outdoor ad, a small design
upon the grand. We might as well

have called the moon American, and raised
a dollar sign above the silver land.

Primate Song

The book, the purse, the door—
the objects differ but the verb
remains the same. It's open.
Signs are made with hands,
a word means a banana, and the chimps
are all American. So now what
are you wanting? More more more.

Of all of Washoe's kids there's one
named Lewis, whom the scientists decided
not to sign to. How does Lewis feel?
We too have hands, we ought to know.
Some signs he learns from other monkeys
but not all. The rest agree. Who's that
there in the mirror? Me me me.

Inflation

Language wasn't any
funny money I was playing with,
no toy surprise, no watch or wooden
nickel, not
a nickel nickel either, twice
removed, sign of a sign.
I meant to make
so deep a song

it held no end of love.
But now I'm dumb
to frame the stream
of stills I feel,
stuck in the onrush without any
one that I was singing to,
without a you, and currents go on running up
a bill of silver senselessness—the seconds counted
in the hundreds, in the thousands, in the billions, till the till

is burst. Remember how enormous one
old swollen moment used to be?
Remember how we loved
position 99, the one where you
look forward? Man, as I look back, I wonder how

did numb get so comparative?
How did the verb to come
(our childhood's bright
infinitive) become
so narrow a necessity?

To Have To

is an odd infinitive, in which
compulsion and possession meet
and share a word together.

Both propose, and both accept;
to have because it wants to hold;
have to, because it has no will.

But then there is
no past or present either.
Coming's going, in this match.

It's odd because they're one
and endless, in the end, in their
capacity to be attached . . .

At Sprecht Academy

we saw the water rising, but could not get through
to headmaster or dean, known to prefer
more spiritual matters: Henshaw for example never cared
what color the coffee mugs were, though Dora the kitchen girl
loved their eggshell sheen and stony heft; nor did DeVito quite
    admire
the shape of Verna's hair, which shone in spikes out from her head
like models of the saints or planets; no one in authority
would notice any straight-C kid with any
knack for knots, the one beginning bookkeeper who dreamt
of non-denominations. Let the world be full
of notabilities, the bosses thought, that's what
academies are for, to send
the statesmen up and know the Pope and pipe the latest
pop psychology straight to the heart
of the fake red telephone and blah
blah blah. For all I know you're

passing over on a plane right now—could you
by any stretch of the
imagination condescend?
José, who was the first to say
the lit-crit teacher had tin ears,
begins to wail of love and death whenever water
gets above his knees; and Erica, our most
myopic, looks
so serious her glasses flash. She has
no memory, no name for metaphor. But something's
more important, when a people's lost at sea—why else

was your attention caught? What history of literature can claim
the smallest mirror's bright capacity?

Autobiography with Suspended Period

In company obedient but free alone
I overgrew my crop of private yard—I tried
words, worked words, riddled, wed
the worst of them, trained
predicates up trellises, turned
phrases on their twine. Strict liberties
I took, ideas of time; I felt
I could foretell and then
forgot an awful lot. Against
the contraceptive suburb, over every
cellblock, I sent out
the ivy of an invitation;
overfed, I could afford
to toy my heart out on the male
of my imagination, deeply
uncorrected by a man.

I must have had a father but
the money issuing from him
remained unspeakable as sperm,
it was the custom; every dawn
he disappeared, not to return
until an hour of his bed. To make my own
invisibility, I took
a spoon of hoopla, and a little humbug soup,
some foam and folderol; I did
at length apply the brushes,
red and purple, then
at length my lips
to the root (where human

comes from humus). Philophile, I fear
that dirt's too short a word for it:
I whistled for death's dog, Fido
the First, to love the devil
out of him. I spoke, in other words
to slick my luck, to work the second

surfaces and spin
the wheels of please and grease.
All semblances began to fuse—the enterprise
grew dangerously easy. (Cover everything
that's missing, and it could
be you, or more,
idolatrous.) God knows

we talk too much. The ends
of life are rich, it's only
explanation that grows poor . . .

No Place

Identifying myself
with a star or a siren,
a number or stripe, or
a stripe and a star,

mistaking actors and policemen for
their uniforms, and drilling
memory with rectitudes
in empty rooms, in perfect unison, alone

what did I know? Experience would teach me
what no classroom could: to set aside
the *summa cum laude,* give up all
my favorite ultimata (there is one

most beautiful, and one most true;
who could she be? I grilled
the girl in glass). I couldn't rise
until I fell from favor,

couldn't know
by placing what I knew.
I'd never see until I freed the sky
from my idea of

first and last and highest,
taking from it (taking
from my eyes)
the ribbons blinding everything with blue.

The Lyricist's Lament

I never learned the trick of snaps, got sick
on canapés and wit, could never open up
somebody else's rented suit to find
the real gorilla underneath. I missed

the point of alligator shoes,
odd monikers and utter individuals,
and even Lulu Obligata's last soirée
was lost on me. Within an hour I could see

constituent millennia but not a second,
in myself a whole society but not
a single you. (We lyricists are like
to stay home typing up

the sub-groups of the lyric self, beloved
admiral of all our mirrors.) Maybe this

is love asleep, love slumming, love
where sub- and object cannot be

distinguished, love in which it's just
too easy being true.

The Oven Loves the TV Set

Stuck on the fridge, our favorite pin-up girl
is anorexic. On the radio we have a riff

of Muzak sax, and on the mind
a self-help book. We sprawl all evening, all

alone, in an unraised ranch;
all day the company we kept

kept on incorporating. As for worlds
of poverty, we do our best, thanks

to a fund of Christian feeling
and mementos from

Amelia, the foster child, who has
the rags and seven photogenic sisters we require

in someone to be saved. She's proof
Americans have got a heart

to go with all that happy
acumen you read about. We love

a million little prettinesses,
decency, and ribbons on

the cockapoo. But who
will study alphabets for hands? Who gives

a damn what goes into
a good wheelchair? Who lugs the rice

from its umpteen stores
to the ends of the earth, to even one

dead-end? Not we.
Our constitutional pursuit

is happiness, i.e.
somebody nice, and not

too fat, we can have
for our personal friend.

Unfamiliar

The foreign filmmaker cannot
explain his images. Two women
kneel in a garden, their hands
and shadows of their hands
flow over soil and seedling;
sometimes shadows meet and then
enormous stemming, branching, leaving
comes to mind. The women go
indoors to stand
by windows they've made green.
The camera dwells
on the doorknob where
a hand rests, taking shape.

The foreign filmmaker is asked
to say a few words on his art.
Where was he going? I explore
one area, he says (it sounds
like "aria") and then
another; I don't see it

as progression. Overhead a large
clock, institutional, means
nothing suddenly, washing
its face with its hands.
Whose land

is this? I can't
explain myself.
Looking for anything I know
I focus on the window
of the classroom. Once it held
a cemetery at a distance;
now it is completely overgrown . . .

Artifactual

All things seem thin
to me, all
things, the cast
and thrown, the pot
and suit of armor,
monarchies in millimeters,
gold in lids. O held
divinity! All
iconography is scrip.

All proper pronouns
in department stores,
suspended periods in hospitals,
thin things!
The skin, the very
thought of skin! The spike
in the EKG or mickey
in the mainstream (lumps
administered as money,
pound's own part
of speech)—what's
free? No love, on no
account. Our health

is poor, our living's
barely made, it isn't
paradise we lose, we lose
the world. In graveyards
what is being
fenced? As for the promised

lands, those arguments
for settlements,
it seems they're always
bursting at the clasp—
the precious stones

fly off, disguised
as stars, loved ones
are lost. Where words aren't free

the heart grows poor. In our
defense, what can
we swear upon?
The life of us
we can't do something for?
The death we can't do anything against?

We Had Words

We sent on the ship a picture
of ourselves, naked, thinking

sex better be on the up-and-up out there
(though here on earth no one may mention

words for privates proper).
Enclosing nine by twelves of

male and female and the galaxy, we meant to show
how we're disposed to everything. (But from

what angle will they read our map? And with
what eyes? How could the brightest of the otherworldly tell

Orion from Adam?) Human beings think
their river-loving, gravity-ridden, sun-adjusted selves are in

the stars, as far as futures go. They think they're smart, and
    space will need
some spatial reasoning, some special ed. (But take it from an
    expert—all

the universities on earth aren't wide enough
to comprehend a single cell. How strike out

on a raft of self, into the blue, wielding a stick
of absolutes, when even it

is hewn of human fears? When languages
are littler than life, and just

between two lovers like ourselves
the distances are years?)

Who Made Her

She is half who made her.—WALLACE STEVENS

*

You put the house about my body,
stud by stud and space by space,
till it seemed all
the frame a freedom needed,

twelve stars in a window more
than any universe at large.
You made room in the world for me,
four rooms, to be

exact, the number
of chambers made
to beat.

*

So screw good manners.
There's no nice
prim syntax for
the baby's loss—the wailing comes

as utter unbecoming, pain
from brainpan, rocks
from voice box, sex
from the confessional, my god,
how could you disappear?

*

In Chinese scrolls the lovers curl
around each other for millennia,
and babies are forever being made
with perfect little parents in their cells;
a carpenter constructs a house of hope
inside the house of pine. Mine too,
I thought the joiner's art.
But now I see my song has issued

never from the cool remove—no love
of each thing in its place, no bed or bank
against the rushes, nothing toward
about a boat, no where or way
to steer it. Lord, you
made me, made me, made me
goes the song (but can you hear it?
all that blame and praise
inseparable?) I loved you both

in throes and theory,
in spasms and in spirit.

Earthmoving Malediction

Bulldoze the bed where we made love,
bulldoze the goddamn room.
Let rubble be our evidence
and wreck our home.

I can't give touching up
by inches, can't give beating
up by heart. So set the comforter
on fire, and turn the dirt

to some advantage—palaces of pigweed,
treasuries of turd. The fist
will vindicate the hand,
and tooth and nail

refuse to burn, and I
must not look back, as Mrs. Lot
was named for such a little—
something in a cemetery,

or a man. Bulldoze the coupled
ploys away, the cute exclusives
in the social mall. We dwell

on earth, where beds
are brown, where swoops
are fell. Bulldoze

the pearly gates:
if paradise comes down
there is no hell.

It Is Unhealthy Not to Die

So why am I amazed
amends cannot be made, amazed
things actually get
beyond repair, amazed a love
breaks down, until no rope or wrench
or jack can patch it up, O maker of all
I love and study, why make me
amazed at your old aptitudes
for hooking spirit up to letter or
ineffable to manifest,
and going matched to coming, god,
and stops to all our bargains with beginning.
Making up a maker, having called
for pet superlatives, dubbing someone
best or ultimate or only or
most reverend, we made
our bed. I didn't mean
to lie, but what to say
came first, once first
is said to come? Did someone really have
no belly button once? Wasn't the apple a bullet,
once she bit it? Here's

to his health, and to her
health, and to
my solitary own—some mud
in the human eye whose red
is otherwise so naked.

Where

I leave the drink and cigarette
where the music is, and go
outdoors where nothing
is the whole idea (where winter
zeros in on eyes and orphans
everyone, and clear is not a kind
of thought). Outside in other words you're not

as gone as in a house.
(Remember the painting called
"The Empty Chair"? It showed
two chairs, identical
except that one contained a hat.
Which is the empty chair, I asked.
You thought the question trivial.
I thought the hat

an extra emptiness.) Between "a room"
and "room" you didn't
mark the article of difference. The knife
fell on the bed, a ruler we had on hand.
I must have missed you when I was

the one that I was thinking of.
I came inside again and left
the feeling in the glove.

ID

Did I? Is it? Hit
below the belt, the ego

doesn't know the difference,
KO, OK, ego can't

identify its problems, can't
identify itself. O

cogito, it says, O sum.
And then, in its cape,

freed from the pay phone, who
says I have come, and in the name

of whom? Someone's living in here,
somewhere deep inside, but still

the elevator's stuck, the clock is slow,
the news is yellow in the hallway stack,

the ego's middle name is mud—there's
trouble in 4A and now

there's trouble in 2B; the plumbing
leaks, a hole is in the head, and tell me

how did all this happen?
Is the super dead?

Gospel According to Virginia

The devil lived, or else
there could have been no holiness.
I learned my etiquette

from Miss Aimée, who kept
a mystery inside the barn, her moron son;
he fumbled at the lip of senses, had

a padlock for a rattle. Left alone
five minutes with the neighbor's baby, I
encouraged it to cry, I pinched it

just to study cause. In hurricanes we knelt and sang
while laws were broken, branches,
glass. In other counties, kids

had heads unnaturally large, like 4-H melons;
did their mothers fall
in love with their uncles? At least there was

love. Between the towns, the fields
were scrap straw stuck in mud; the wind went in
and out of women's dresses. God invented oyster shells

to pave the road, to feed the hen, to spread
the word about pearl. The cat
caught sight of us

and split— What's there
but two roads crossing? All I know
of my mother's loneliness was once—

scared of the lone man watching us, who leaned
against a tree and chewed weed—she (for whom
the good and true were not synonymous)

got us the hell out of there.

Hole Filler

The cat is killed
by the passionate petter,
the poem by clappers who mob
its best-laid calms, and looks
are eaten up entirely by beloveds,
apples no one wanted once
the worm had had his fill.
From happiness and hurt
in equal parts the lovers cry;
as for the gigolo, he has
an eye for what?
An eye.

Earmarks

In time-lapse film the flowers yearn and sway
in ways we find too suddenly
familiar, pumping
in and out all month, and surging
toward the bloomingest of health and then
collapsing, falling off;

the solid calcium we laid
beneath the new electron microscope
is made it now appears
of lace and air.
For bridges lie in bones,
and revolutions in a rose,
the world breathes in, breathes out,

each unity turns out to be
a part, each part appears from
somewhere else the sum; the thought
of comprehending can itself
be comprehended (something's always
bigger than the thought);
you don't have to be smart

to be *able* to wipe the world away;
and you have to be stupid to do it.
So now the question is how close
is rot to ripe? Upon
the universe of animals I swear
I mean I think I mean
I pray we are a stripe.

Our Element

Water fills the drain with *raison d'être,*
eloquence of artery and ditch—
the force of field and soul
of rationality—cool-headed,

looking to be level. Water writes
the pipe's sonata, plays
the gravel's rattle, goes
post-haste for bays (big water, as

the baby says, while little waters lap
in backyard wading pools) and all
the water in the world is wound
from some big spool in heaven, bound

for sewers, bound for brown, but made
for thoughts of silver bolt, an endless silk
insurgency; we cut such minor
figures from it, in it, via

banks and clefs and PVC; but water wishes
every obstacle away, it dreams of skirting
earth in ocean, dreams of scarfing
sky in cloud; and even down and out don't seem

so different in this centrifuge
with melted mountains at
its heart, and fire and water
welded in a wheel—for love

is made for gravity; if we
weren't stuck on earth, where would we get
our sense of flight? Why have the funny
flats of feet at all,

or bounce, or beat,
or heart and lungs hung up
in red felt rooms? The beauty of
the breast and balls

is heft: the curve of every
loveliness depends
from cord and tendon,
spine and wire, until

we can't hold up
another day. Are finally,
are fatally, attracted
to the bed. From there

the human beings look
so tall! The stars appear
no further off than glances—see?
Your closest friend has blinked an eye

and miles of silver fall . . .

Forecast

Later the ferryboats will come,
bedecked with hundreds
hot from city jobs to pass (or maybe not
to pass, in bright pink jogging shorts
and reddish spectacles) for the
perennially idle, known
to idle here. The beaches allocated to the public
will have turned into a cityscape by ten,
with suburbs of umbrellas, brass from cans,
the waft of bubblegum and coconut,
a year of work redeemable
in one weekend. (And that is what
becomes of time, wherever time is money.) Still

for now, it's five AM, before the break
of day, before a soul would even think
to subdivide the sun, and mourning doves are casting old
consoling silvers down from trees, and even last night's trash is
    washed
by cool light in the street. In this café, unhurried, one can find
a steadiness of commonplaces to be grateful for: the coffee's
regular (as sure as shit, Maggie would say); the sweetpea
winding back and forth along
the cordwork of a southern window
testifies to minor lights and little luxuries;
the baby has a piece of toast. It's all her own.
At six AM each day McMann, who's eighty-two,
stoops at the café window to retrieve
the same blue plastic milkcrate from the gutter
where each night it's tossed; as careful as a diamond-cutter
he will reposition it against the wall.
A purple latticework falls out from sun
and this arrangement, onto reddish masonry: the shadow
makes a most amazing lace—*memento avenir* and fluid
graph—a map that moves. It's

seven-thirty, suddenly, it's ten.
McMann is gone; the shadow's grid
(that mind to move, made fast, sun-made)
is gliding overtop the grid of bricks
(that mind to stay, made fast, man-made).
Which world is real? The day

wears on, the people
pass, and substance only seems
a blueprint to the shade . . .

IV

Shades

The day shines down in waves
and particles. The Sunday patrons of the open-air café
are shimmering—their eyelids, earlobes, orbits all
isosceles-bespangled.
Over obligato streams
of car-sparkle arise
the brilliant disquisitions of
the fork on plate, the baby's whoop
for brief on human happiness, and there
above the five-and-dime, against
an empty blue (or is it just
the eye that's uninhabited?) the pure

line of a spire. What more could we want
than this world, sharpened by shine and dark,
facetted by accident, anchored
by appearance? Well, we could want

the dead to be with us again,
be with us still—be somehow
undiminished, unbegun, so we
won't die the way we fear (they could be here,
in all the carnivals of cups and trade,
with faces chance might turn to ours,
in sympathy, in mirrored shades . . .)

But no. The world makes
too much of itself. No sense allowed
beyond the five—it's blinding, deafening,
demanding, and alive. A thousand diamonds splinter out
from fender, windshield, chrome—a spray
of glints, a glance of blades.
The human being, struck, can just
put darker glasses on.

Spilled

The waiter dropped a tray of glassware and
the din of conversation stopped as if
in shock at competition. Not until
that moment were we quite aware

of what a roar the ordinary made,
not until a knife of other noise could cut
right through it to the greater emptiness,
right through to zero, there

where no one for a moment said
a blessed word. And then the other
nothings started coming back, the hum of small talk
rising gradually to flow and to recirculate, its rhythms

swelling up and out of the hole in the story to make
the story normal once again, the cruise control back on,
the life as a career in which we can afford,
as usual, to fail to hear.

*

The restaurant's a show of selves
collected into dreamy twos and fours;
their fantasies are fed, their livings made;
the hundred couples can pretend

they are accustomed to a cook and maid
and then, by some consensual agreement (because none
can really be the monarch of the model) they ignore
the commonplace, with its proximities, the many

foreign monarchies that munch and belch
next door. Each buys a little
privacy, say three by five, and dreams that he
is different. The dream is purchased at the price

of never seeing being from above or from
a distance, somewhere difference might disappear,
and all of what is being said
might add up to one animal's

far-flung identifying cry: for all we know
that's how a God is reached, in whose
broad synaesthesias of sympathy a blood
need not be bright or red if spilled as speech . . .

A Mother

It hurts, inside, as if inside there really were
a famous place for feelings, called
the heart. How make it better, take it

back? The judges
stuff their ears but still
their eyes are sharp—I see, they say,

whose very teeth can glance, whose shelves are full
of corneas in jars. They rule
the apple's Adam's, whereas Eve

must brood (who had no mother
and who has to bear
both murderer and murderee). At night

the voice gets through
the telephone's umbilicus. It's
grieving and it's craving and

I'll never get away.
Why did you leave,
the ones who made us say.

Not a Sin

It's not a virtue either, really, this
rubbing and rubbing against
someone, yourself
a someone too, until
someone must burst or yell. It falls

where pleasure and necessity and risk
all intersect—we have ourselves and
to ourselves, to love, and half to death—
removing, move by move,
the overlays of mind until

we're down to sheer medulla—not
what you would call intelligent, and yet
I bet it has some wisdom in it, something that can bear us
later, past
the lapse in gushes, past the businesses part,
past weeks and decades made to keep
our waking occupied, till when

one moment yawns no memory foretold,
one end of time no wording
comprehends, reducing
all our big ideas
to jolts of oblongata, oh

my underestimated God, shall I
show forth thy praise? You made
my powers crash. As bushes burst,
as flames float off
in heart-boats, in the flood,
I open up my mouth and find
you've filled it full of flesh—I mean

you made me feel
the way I feel
so words would not be proud. I know.
You made men so I'd kneel.

In Primary Colors

I like it like it
is. It may
be artless, may
be ungrammatical, the car
be stuck but still I say
the passengers can sing.
The song's the luster's
and I need you now, this
ample moment, not
as afterthought or for
forebearing, here and
now, in this
sunlit back seat—
and fuck your
fessors, pro and con,
and fuck appointments with
accountants, many miles to go before
the tongue and tail are fully
forked. Look out, the city's
hot on everybody's
heels, the lions are taking
the sun on the library steps
and books are bound
for nowhere, in bright cloth.
On the tip of my tongue
I like your tongue, I
like it like it
is. The eyes are bright
in the lowly shoe,
good turns are done
in belt and cuff; where did
we think to go? Just
like it like it
is, just so, just
feel till you feel felt.

The Typewriter's the Kind

The typewriter's the kind
of heavy gray that's good
for leaning on. I sit
in front of it with holes

torn in my meanings, or a heart
so full of complication I can't even
start to start, and on
the radio the cello's

unaccompanied, and on the hour
the news is *entendu;* I lay my arms
upon the typewriter, my head
upon my arms, and breathe

and breathe and breathe and there
is all the cool immutability
a fevered human needs,
its current humming constant like

the speed of light or fact
of water (there is death
on earth this moment, there
is death on earth this moment. Always

is already). Then
I can get up and mend
and celebrate and see
the endless world's unsavability.

Hard

Suppose you have
to move a mountain.
Do you call up All-or-Nothing Limited
with blasters in battalions, and dispatch
the under- and the other-worldly straight
to smithereens?

A moment blows
what several thousand years could ease—
time moves the planet all the time without
demolishing the delicate—no opposition
between powers, no antipathy
of east to west. The networks go

so far and fine we can't
conceive them—intricacies of a single
rock or river, rate of rainbow—look,
I can't get over it. Let all your big
bulldozing eras
snore their fast Manhattans down;

let lovers of the good and quick
erect their clever rocks (the graveyard has
its own downtown); let book ends wind up being all
our reason for the books, and men learn only yes and no
in other people's languages (believe
no code but cracked). Perhaps their wills

need execution often.
I have harder
work to do,
a teardrop at
a time until
the whole world's stoneworks soften.

Melted Money

Time and time again
we told them not to leave
their stuff so near the stove.
But children have no past and so
they don't believe in futures.
Whiles and whiles
of smoke unwind
from houses, causing
more or less sky, I
can't tell. I spent

my life forgetting how
a music pours right off
the measured page, and intuition
floods the calendar, and animals
go stitching our enumerated
yards together, world already
without end. A little

gold spills out from windows in
the neighborhood (has everybody spent
too much on God's next birthday?). Thanks
to the invisible, we are alive. Take
heat—you can't directly
see it, but it spins
a shadow on the floor as clear
as any cast by iron stove—it is
the meaning of the stove, and moving
off from it. The children now

are nowhere to be seen;
the children's pictures
look undone. And already
flesh-colored crayons begin
to melt into earth-colored ones . . .

Labor

Each sword of the plant is burning.
You would not believe
what surgery midwinter light
can do, cutting

subject from object. I don't want
the way I used to, rushing to have
and swallow whole. Death takes
its time; little by little

I've lost my taste for victory.
Let others fight for rank and class.
I pass. It's better
plants and stars prevail

without our interloping,
eyes for certitude and arms for law,
our pens for poor
taxonomy, our

campaign promises and rant.
Too long has love
been taken for
belonging—

let it fall away.
I have to carry
water now.
I need to feed the plant.

Stairwell

The telescope's a microscope,
the stars are in our eyes, and not
all orders come from somewhere
you could call above.

Rivers of money, streams of time,
the currents have a twist
of DNA; if terminals permit
our powers here to flow or fail,

those terminals are far
or future ones. What makes us dead
can make a rail alive. I swear
it was a wisdom in my dream that spoke

like nothing in a story, no
two sides to every time,
no pitch or tempo to the utterance, when it
said death was in a second. It meant

IN—not soon, not carpe diem, not another time—
but now, far in, where space and time
are not to ends. Despite
the boundaries between

named space and naming men,
no God is nailed to knowledge (that's
the trouble with the tree); no wise
is nailed to where, no way

to when. We made our minds up, now
they cannot understand. (You don't
catch waves using a net.) There is no future
in some languages. We could

be dead already, don't forget.

Two Humans Being

The street's awash with city life,
the overflow from bookstores, undertow
from magic, marketplace of goods and good,
act and idea. A person tells
a fortune for a quarter, and
another fashions riddles from
the letters of the customer's last name; a third
hawks necklaces of tooth and bone; there's food
from thirteen cultures, sunshine from
a hundred years away.
From my position

(at the coffee-counter where
I've paused for speed, quick fix
in transient life) two people
in the thick of this, two beings
in the protoplastic mass, appear
unguised. One is an infant
in her mother's arms—sun-flooded
near the café window, skin a virtual
transparency (where is
she *from?*)—her veins and bones
illuminated, she's a brilliant
piece of work. She cannot take

her gaze away
from the tinted throng; her eyes must be
amazed. (Perhaps the past's
ahead, and heaven underfoot.)
Into her purview comes
the other unself-conscious one,
a woman maybe sixty-five, with
trousers patched together under skirts,
coats under shawls, a person wearing
everything she owns. She passes by and waves
a wand of bubbles! Now
the baby's look is naked,
wonderstruck—what

miracles of simple
soap and water! Shades I had
forgotten for three decades
swim upon my sight and rise—
the blues undimmed by bodily attachment,
purples straight from paradise, and clear
unmitigated green—each bubble is a world

of pure appearance, every one endowed
with tiny street and crowd,
café and baby,
seer and seen . . .

With You Gone

For Wydette, with love

We see signs everywhere—the stars
and stones are moving, every
animal is you. Don't
slap that fly, says Connie, and we all
laugh outright, after all week weeping.
You are there, in the hilarity itself,
in us (Steve has your face
and walk, and Scott your kind
of kindnesses and doubt, and Mary moral
eloquence, and Charles your sense
of solitude and the sensational,
and Connie's funny and your parents share
their home with me, someone they barely know.
I read your scrawl, I write the record, cannot speak
enough for you). It's we

who are the missing ones, the way
a person in a mirror stares
forever, without being there. Who are we like?
What do we know? The race is
20 miles per second, every day around
a nuclear event or local politics or fashionable interior
    and then

one's brother cannot breathe. Millennia

are dust. We cannot locate you; we're lost.
That's why we're sitting here
at midnight, on the curb
outside your parents' house,
struck dumb, our cigarettes
a little constellation.
All around us, stars
pour down. In amniotic blue
the earth is curled. We love you
suddenly so much we feel
out of this world . . .

As It Was in the Beginning

*

As soon as you say moon and stars
you lose their oddity and wallop.
Most of what exists
is otherworldly, but as soon

as you say wonderful no wonder's
in it; awful seems so small
compared to awe. Who dared give God
a proper name?

*

As soon as you say you, you have
a crowd. Hard to keep deep enough
by rote or rule. Keep deep inside—
let Rigel be the ring on your own

left foot, the shine on the knife
sent from before
the New World was. It's
lonely lonely lonely

here on earth. As soon as you say like, you sear
a trail across the sky-brain—like means likes
of us. Now who shall we call different?
(The animals die first and then

the human vegetables,
mon petit chou.)

*

As soon as you say now
the past can end. My friend cannot
stop dying while I live, I won't
let go. In mere binoculars there is

another universe, and better than a sword
Orion has a nebula! What can we see,
our eyes a blur? I hope I don't
hate death, or live

too small a life. For though I lose it
let me not deny it (even as
a muffling brilliance falls
on posts and on positions in the night,

along the city limits, both sides of
the neighbor's fence, soft
centuries of snow.
And everything falls quiet).

Thought of Night

Just think of it,
and you surround it with

its opposite. Take here
and now, for instance. Do we see

a line where there is none? We draw
up sides, forgetting how in cells

division made things whole. To me
I'm complete, but I'm partial to you.

*

So as we fall
into the night (which isn't, after all

is said and done, the opposite
of day) I cannot see

our differences. Love mends
the broken language—we are each

first persons (though I know
I mustn't speak for two). I only mean

I feel myself again, inside,
and it is you.

How Come: A Book of Numbers

1
What brought us here? A boat
and a wish. How do we know?
In every sense. The five
are fast and shallow and
the six are long and deep.
Where do men keep the time they keep?
And who has space? In twenty
little centuries. A man
is in the moon.

2
Of all the questions, motive
is the hardest one to learn, the last
to lose. When children get it

it's a magic automatic:
why why why, provoking our
because because because. The thinkers think it

everything; the old know best. They ask us
What's the question, What's the question,
till we call them deaf.

3
Deep in the brain we keep
a hypothalamus, a little
jilted planet. There, despite
the history of causes (square house,
long bow, numbing multiples of arms, the arguments for why
this was, or that) there's something we
can't run, or gun, or find the owner of.
It can't absolve, but it is said
to soothe. At night, we climb in there and dream,
released from reason. Then the boat
begins to move.

From 20,000 Feet

The cloud formation looks
like banks of rock from here
though rock and cloud are thought

so opposite. Earth's underlying
nature might be likeness—
likeness everywhere disguised

by wave-length, amplitude and frequency.
(If we got far enough away could we
decipher the design?) From here

so much goes by
too fast or slow
for sight. (Is death

a stretch of time
in which a life is just
a flash?) Whatever we may think we only

think that we will lose. The foetus,
expert at attachment, didn't dream
that cramped canal would open

into sound and light and love—
it clung. It didn't care.
The future looked like death to it, from there.

About the author

Heather McHugh divides her life between urban university life and rural nature, west and east coasts. She is a professor in the M.F.A. program at the University of Washington, Seattle, and in 1987 was Holloway lecturer at the University of California, Berkeley. She lives half of the year in Eastport, a small island community in Maine.

McHugh is a graduate of Harvard University (Radcliffe College, B.A. 1970) and the University of Denver (M.A. 1972). She has taught at Columbia University, the University of California, Irvine, and SUNY Binghamton. She is a continuing member of the M.F.A. Program for Writers at Warren Wilson College. She has received grants from the National Endowment for the Arts and from the New York State Arts Council. Her earlier books are *Dangers, A World of Difference,* and *To the Quick* (Wesleyan 1987), and a translation of the poems of Jean Follain, *D'Après Tout.*

About the book

Shades was composed in Meridien by G & S Typesetters, Inc. of Austin, Texas. The design is by Kachergis Book Design, Inc. of Pittsboro, North Carolina.

WESLEYAN UNIVERSITY PRESS 1988